The Baby who Changed the World.

written by **Sheryl Ann Crawford**

illustrated by **Sonya Wilson**

A Faith Parenting Guide can be found on page 32.

Faith Kids is an imprint of Cook Communications Ministries, Colorado Springs, CO 80918
Cook Communications, Paris, Ontario
Kingsway Communications, Eastbourne, England

THE BABY WHO CHANGED THE WORLD
© 2000 by Sheryl Ann Crawford for text and by Sonya Wilson for illustrations.

Faith Kids™ is a registered trademark of Cook Communications Ministries.

Scripture quotation is taken from the *International Children's Bible, New Century Version*, copyright © 1983, 1986, 1988 by Word Publishing, Dallas, Texas 75039. Used by permission.

Edited by Leon C. Wirth
Designed by PS Marketing Communications

First printing, 2000
Printed in Singapore
04 03 02 01 00   5 4 3 2 1

Presented to:

_____

By:

_____

Date:

_____

"A child will be born to us.
God will give a son to us.
He will be responsible for
leading the people.
His name will be Wonderful Counselor,
Powerful God,
Father Who Lives Forever,
Prince of Peace."

Isaiah 9:6 (ICB)

Imagine what these words might have
meant before the first Christmas,
before this special baby was born. Imagine how
some might have wondered just what kind
of special baby could possibly be all these
wonderful things . . .
. . . a baby who would change the world!

The following story is based on Luke 2:1-20.

A tired donkey has
arrived in a stable in
the town of Bethlehem,
with some interesting news
for his new friends . . .

"A baaaby? Did you say a baaaby is coming?" asked Sheep.

"That's right," said Donkey. "A baby who will change the world."

Donkey lay down on a mound of hay and heaved a sigh of relief.

"Ahhhhh. My poor, aching hooves need a rest," he quietly moaned.

A cow, munching hay from the manger, lifted her head in surprise. "But, Donkey, what can a baby do to change the world?" she asked softly.

"This baby is very special," said Donkey. "There's never been a baby like this one. And," whispered Donkey, "I think He's going to be born in our stable tonight!"

"A baby in our stable?" asked Cow. "How wonderful!"

Donkey's excited eyes grew wide. "Yes! And this baby will grow up to be a powerful king! He'll be absolutely perfect, pure, and spotless. He's been called the Prince of Peace and Wonderful Counselor."

"Wow!" cried Cow.

"Amaaaaazing," bleated Sheep.

"It sure is, and listen to this . . . ," Donkey tried to continue.

"I have a question!" pronounced a deep, proud voice from the corner of the stable. Big, strong Ox stepped out of the shadows. "Did you say a baby is coming who will change the world, and that He'll be a powerful king?" asked Ox.

"Yes! That's right!" said Donkey. "And . . ."

"Well then," interrupted Ox, "I expect He'll be a baby ox. You've heard the saying 'he's as strong as an ox,' haven't you?" he asked no one in particular.

9

Ox grinned wide, but the animals . . .

except for Donkey . . . laughed loud and
long at the thought of an Ox king.

"That's the silliest thing I've ever
heard!" Cow cackled.

Sheep stood up proudly. "Besides, you
heard Donkey say this baby will be pure
and spotless . . . just like a white, fluffy
newborn lamb!"

Donkey tried to continue, "Sure, but this baby . . ."

"This baaaby who will change the world," Sheep cut in,

"must certainly be a lamb!"

"His majesty, the Lamb? Think again!" Ox laughed so hard his sides hurt.

"Hee hee hee, that's funny to me!" laughed Cow.

Sheep, however, didn't think it was funny at all.

As the laughter quieted, a dove gracefully glided down from the rafters.

"Pardon me," said Dove. "I distinctly heard that this baby will be the Prince of Peace! Since doves have always stood for peace, this baby cooo-cooo-could be a baby dove!"

This time, the animals roared with laughter. But Donkey just shook his head sadly.

Cow, giving Ox and Sheep a nudge, stepped forward. "This idea of a baby who can change the world really moooooooves me. You said this baby would be called 'Wonderful.' What's more wonderful than a newborn calf?"

All the animals, except for Cow, fell to the ground with laughter, and even Donkey cracked a brief smile.

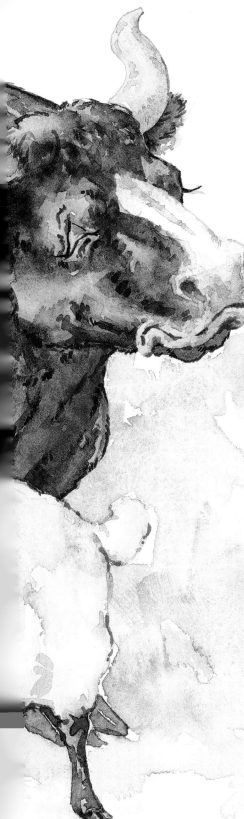

"No, no, no! Wrong, wrong, WRONG!" Donkey declared above the laughter. With that, the animals stopped in stunned silence.

"It's not an ox, though oxen are strong. It's not a lamb, though lambs are beautiful. It's not a dove, though doves do remind everyone of peace. And it's not a calf, though I have met some wonderful calves." The animals sighed with disappointment.

"I suppose you're going to tell us it's a baby donkey," said Cow quietly under her breath.

"No," Donkey sighed. "This baby who will change the world, as amazing as it sounds, will be a baby *human*."

"A baby human?" The animals gasped!

"Yes," Donkey replied. "A baby human boy."

Dove flapped her wings in alarm. "But how? No human is perfect. They do wrong things all the time!"

"Yes, humans are full of sin," claimed Cow. "They're all born with it."

Ox snorted! "And it keeps them away from the Creator, because they can't make up for those sins."

"Humans are baaaaad!" Sheep insisted. "No sinful human can make up for a sinful world!"

"It's impossible!" Ox exclaimed. "It's ridiculous!" Dove cried.

"I refuse to believe it!" Sheep huffed.

"You made that up!" Cow accused Donkey.

Donkey stood firm, switching his tail with excitement. "But this is no ordinary baby boy! This baby is really God's own Son coming from Heaven!"

"God's Son? Coming here?!" they said.

"Yes!" Donkey said, almost dancing with excitement. "And because He's God's perfect Son, He can't and won't do anything wrong." Together the animals looked up in the sky and noticed the brightest star ever, sparkling high above them.

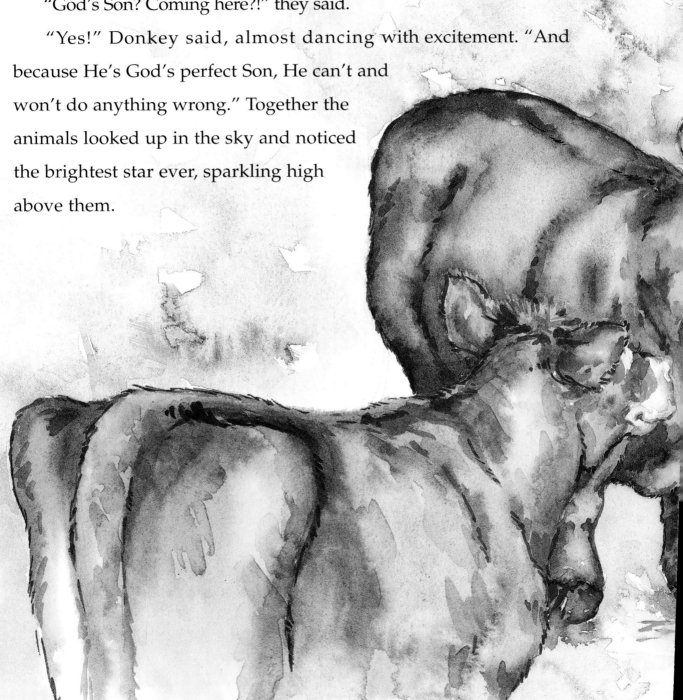

Donkey's tail switched faster. "I even know His name," he whispered. "It's the most beautiful name I've ever heard." He began to spell out a name in the dirt, with his hoof. J-E-S-U-S.

The animals whispered the name over and over, "Jesus. Jesus. Jesus."

"God gave Him that name. It means 'Savior'," said Donkey. "He's going to save humans from their sins."

"Jesus," Dove cooed quietly. "It is a lovely name, indeed."

" Jesus," Sheep sighed happily. "It is a beautiful name."

"JESUS !" Ox bellowed. "I like the sound of it. It's a strong name!"

"But, how " Cow questioned, "could God's Son save them?"

18

Silently, Donkey turned around and began to spell out another word on the dirt floor with his hoof. L-O-V-E.

"LOVE," said Donkey. "Love will help Him forgive them and help them make up with God."

"If you didn't make this up" asked Cow, "how do you know?"

"I walked from a faraway town called Nazareth with a young couple named Joseph and Mary," Donkey explained.

"God chose Mary to be the Mommy for Baby Jesus! Along the way, they talked about the things I've told you! I think He'll be born here, tonight!"

All the animals began talking at once about how fantastic and incredible and exciting it was. Jesus was coming to their stable! They were so excited that they mooed, and cooed, and bleated, and snorted, and pranced, and danced, and then . . . Donkey's ears suddenly popped up in surprise.

"He's coming!" he shouted.

"We know!" they shouted back joyfully.

"No, I mean, Joseph is coming with Mary! Listen!"

Donkey said nervously.

The animals could hear the sound of footsteps approaching.
"Hurry everyone! Let's mooooove," Cow suggested. "Give them all the
room they need!"

The stable door creaked open. The
animals could see Mary leaning on
Joseph's arm.
They stepped
inside and tried to
get comfortable
while the animals
quietly watched in
awe.

22

That night Baby Jesus was born. Mary laid Him in the manger to rest. From the shadows, the happy animals could not take their eyes off God's little Son.

"He's the most beautiful baby I've ever seen," Cow whispered.

"Even for a human," Dove agreed.

"Something's wrong," Ox added, a little too loudly.

"Hush," said Sheep.

"Let's go outside if you need to talk," Donkey suggested.

The animals quietly slipped out of the stable into a beautiful starry night, bathed in light from the brilliant star above. But Ox didn't seem to notice, pacing back and forth.

"I'm worried," Ox huffed. "How will the humans find out about Baby Jesus? There are so many in this great big world!"

"I'm sure the Creator will find a way," Donkey replied. "I don't know how or when, but I'm sure He will."

"LOOK!" Dove cried, flapping her wings.

"We have visitors!"

"This is the place! This is the PLAAAACE! He's got to be here!" an anxious sheep shouted to the others behind her, running as fast as her little legs could go.

"Do you KNOW who's in there?" said the stable animals.

"Yes!" said the shepherd's sheep. "God's special baaaby, the Savior! And you'll never believe what we just saw out in the fields!"

"An angel came out of nowhere and told the shepherds about God's Son; that He was here in this town. Then the night filled with light, and the sky was actually BURSTING with angels praising God! So, we hurried to town looking for the baaaaby, and here He is!"

"Wonderful!" Ox exclaimed. "Humans are finding out that God's Son, the Baby Jesus has come!"

The animals watched as the shepherds left the stable and began to tell others in the little town of Bethlehem.

"It starts here, tonight, my friends," Donkey said. "The story starts here. And who knows how far God will spread this great news!"

And sure enough, travelers in the city of Bethlehem spread the news that God's Son had come to earth! And those that heard the wonderful news and heard about His life through the years began to tell others FAR BEYOND that little stable in Bethlehem . . .

29

. . . far beyond where the
animals in the stable could have
imagined . . . far beyond the cities . . .
far beyond the country . . .

. . . far beyond
the years of time . . .

. . . and now this wonderful news
has reached you!

Yes, a baby was born who
grew up to do what we could
never do by ourselves. He
loves us. He forgives us for all
we've done wrong. And He
helps us make up with God.
And that's what He did.

He's Jesus. The baby who
changed the world!

31

Age: 4-7

Life Issue: Understanding that Jesus came to save the world.

Spiritual Building Block: Christmas/Faith

Learning Styles

Sight: Watch a video or church program which depicts the traditional Christmas story as given in Luke 2. Ask your child, "What makes this baby special? How is this baby different from any other baby? What would this baby do when he grew up that would help everyone?" If time allows, retell the story again or have the child retell the story to you.

Sound: Choose several Christmas carols that your family can sing together. "Away in a Manger" or "Silent Night" are good suggestions. Talk about the meaning of these songs and emphasize the importance of Christ's coming to save all people from sin. If a recording of Handel's Messiah is available, listen to the track "For Unto Us a Child is Born." Even at this age, children will enjoy listening to this wonderful holiday music.

Touch: Pick three or four people that you and your child can tell about the Baby that changed the world—Jesus! Make special Christmas cards that emphasize the Babe in the manger. On the inside, help your child copy Isaiah 9:6. Let him or her sign each card and send them out to people you've chosen. Pray for these people regularly during the holiday season.

"She will give birth to a son, and you are to give him the name Jesus, because he will save his people from their sins."
Matthew 1:21 (NIV)